Native
American
Peoples

ONEIDA

Amy M. Stone

Gareth Stevens Publishing

A WORLD ALMANAC EDUCATION GROUP COMPANY

Please visit our web site at: www.garethstevens.com
For a free color catalog describing Gareth Stevens Publishing's list of high-quality books
and multimedia programs, call 1-800-542-2595 (USA) or 1-800-387-3178 (Canada).
Gareth Stevens Publishing's fax: (414) 332-3567.

Library of Congress Cataloging-in-Publication Data

Stone, Amy, 1947-
    Oneida / by Amy M. Stone.
      p. cm. — (Native American peoples)
    Includes bibliographical references and index.
    ISBN 0-8368-4220-0 (lib. bdg.)
    1. Oneida Indians—History—Juvenile literature. 2. Oneida Indians—
Social life and customs—Juvenile literature. I. Title. II. Series.
E99.O45S86 2004
974.7004'9755—dc22   2004046691

First published in 2005 by
Gareth Stevens Publishing
A World Almanac Education Group Company
330 West Olive Street, Suite 100
Milwaukee, WI 53212 USA

Produced by Discovery Books
Project editor: Valerie J. Weber
Designer and page production: Sabine Beaupré
Photo researcher: Tom Humphrey
Native American consultant: Robert J. Conley, M.A., Former Director of Native American
   Studies at Morningside College and Montana State University
Maps: Stefan Chabluk
Gareth Stevens editorial direction: Mark Sachner
Gareth Stevens art direction: Tammy West
Gareth Stevens production: Jessica Morris

Photo credits: AP/Wide World Photos: cover, pp. 23, 24, 25; Submitted by the Oneida
Nation of Wisconsin: pp. 4 (bottom), 26, 27 (left); Corbis: pp. 5, 8 (bottom), 19, 27 (right);
Native Stock: pp. 6, 7, 8 (top), 12, 14, 15, 16, 18, 20, 21; North Wind Picture Archives: p. 9;
The Oneida Nation Museum of Wisconsin: pp. 11, 13, 17.

Cover caption: This Oneida boy plays an honored part in a ceremony that expresses respect for
Mother Earth and all her creatures. The great protector of the Oneida people, the eagle can
warn of impending danger.

Contents

Words that appear in the glossary are printed in **boldface** type the first time they appear in the text.

Origins

By the early 1600s, the Oneidas occupied and controlled 6 million acres (2.5 million hectares) of land in what is now central New York State.

Through ritual dances like this one, the Oneidas give thanks for the Creator's many gifts.

Lands of the Oneidas

While the Oneidas share a common history, they have followed different paths. About one thousand Oneidas are **enrolled** members of the Oneida Indian **Nation** and live on Oneida homelands near Syracuse, New York. Nearly fifteen thousand Oneidas belong to the Oneida Tribe of Indians of Wisconsin, also called the Oneida Nation of Wisconsin. Tribal members live near Green Bay and Oneida, Wisconsin. The Oneida of the Thames is a rural community of nearly five thousand members in southwestern Ontario, Canada. Three to five thousand Oneidas live on the Six Nations **Reserve** in Ontario, Canada. Other Oneidas live and work throughout the United States and Canada.

Oneida Origins

Like many Indian tribes, Oneidas believe they sprang from the earth and that the Creator made them. Many scientists believe Native Americans' **ancestors** came to North America during the last Ice Age when a landmass may have once connected Asia to what

Language

Today, only a few Oneida elders speak their native language. School- and community-based language programs are helping more people learn to read and write Oneida.

Oneida	Pronunciation	English
e.lhal	ail-hall	dog
takó·s	dah-goes	cat
onhwala	own-wall-ah	caterpillar
aw^.la	ah-wall	green
i.yús	ee-yoos	long
ka'niyús	got-nee-yoos	short

In early summer, the Oneidas' strawberry ceremony honors the healing powers of medicinal plants. Strawberries represent the Oneidas' connection to the earth.

is now Alaska. Others think that Native Americans may have come to the Americas by sea and traveled up from South America.

Oneidas explain their origins in a traditional story, shared with other Iroquois Indians. Before the earth was made, everyone lived happily in the Sky World. One day, Sky Woman tumbled through a hole in this world, crying for help. As she fell, Sky Woman grabbed some strawberry, tobacco, and corn plants. Some of the creatures that lived in the Water World below heard her cries. A loon caught her and put her on the back of a giant sea turtle. Muskrat carried mud in his paws and placed it on turtle's back. Sky Woman transformed into Mother Earth.

When twin boys were born, the "Good Minded" one created edible plants and harmless animals. The other, known as "Dark Minded," created poisonous plants and dangerous animals. The boys fought with each other to see who was most powerful. Good Minded boy won, but it was not a total victory; it was clear the earth would forever be made up of both good and harmful forces.

History

Members of the Iroquois Confederacy

The Mohawk, Onondaga, Cayuga, Seneca, and Oneida Indians lived in what is now New York State and southeastern Canada long before Europeans first encountered them in the early 1600s. As early as the 1400s, Oneida villages spread across nearly 6 million acres (2.5 million hectares) of land in present-day Oneida and Madison Counties in central New York State.

Sacred teachings united the Mohawk, Onondaga, Cayuga, Seneca, and Oneida nations until about the 1100s, when fighting broke out among them. A prophet, the Peacemaker, convinced the nations that warring against each other was foolish. "Because of war," the Peacemaker said, "there is starvation, suffering, and misery. War must cease and everlasting peace must be established

Like other ancient peoples, the Iroquois tied shell beads, or wampum, into patterns that stood for important historical themes. The center object in this wampum belt is the sacred white pine tree, under which the chiefs of the Iroquois Confederacy met in council. The squares on either side of the tree stand for the five confederacy tribes.

among all peoples." Peacemaker taught people rules to live by called the Great Law of Peace. The five nations then formed a **confederacy**. Called the League of the Haudenosaunee (or Iroquois Confederacy), the confederacy later influenced the founding fathers of the United States. It served as a government model that respected its members' independence while promoting justice and equal rights for all.

With endless patience, [Confederacy members] shall carry out their duty. Their firmness shall be tempered with a tenderness for their people. Neither anger nor fury shall find lodging in their minds, and all their words and actions shall be marked by calm deliberation.

From the Great Law of Peace of the League of the Haudenosaunee, or Iroquois

Original Names

Made up of the Oneidas, Mohawks, Onondagas, Cayugas, and Senecas, the Iroquois Confederacy members have always called themselves the Haudenosaunee, meaning "People of the Longhouse," which describes their dwellings. They prefer this name to Iroquois, which is a French term based on Irinakhoiw, the Algonquian Indian word

Called the Haudenosaunee, or People of the Longhouse, the Iroquois covered their houses with the bark of elm trees. A house sheltered several families belonging to the same **clan**.

for the Iroquois. The Oneidas' name for themselves is Onyota'a:ka, which means "People of the Standing Stone." According to Oneida tradition, the Standing Stone appears in each new settlement, guiding the Oneidas' search for fertile lands, water, and other resources. The English explorers of the 1600s called the Onyota'a:ka the Oneida.

During the 1500s and early 1600s, the Oneidas traded furs for European-made metal items such as knives and farming and building tools.

Troubled Times

By the early 1500s, European explorers had arrived in North America. In 1634, measles and smallpox, brought to North America by European traders and settlers, spread throughout the nations of the Iroquois Confederacy. Native Americans had no **immunity** to these diseases, which reduced the Oneida population by two-thirds.

Fighting among the Indians also took a toll. The Iroquois nations had traded animal furs for European trade goods, such as iron pots and pans, knives, and axes. Throughout the late 1600s and early 1700s, however, furs became scarce, which led to wars between the Iroquois Nations and their neighbors, the Huron and Algonquian Nations. Many warriors were killed, further reducing the Iroquois and Oneida population.

During the mid-1700s, Oneida Chieftain Shikellamy crafted treaties with frontier whites that favored the Haudenosaunee, or Iroquois Confederacy, members over the Delaware and Shawnee tribes.

The American Revolution Divides the Confederacy

British colonists who had settled along the eastern coast of North America wanted their independence from Great Britain and started the American Revolution in 1775. At first, many leaders of the Iroquois Confederacy thought the Iroquois Nations should remain **neutral.** Finally, however, the Oneidas, under the leadership of Chief Skenandoah, as well as their friends, the Tuscaroras, sided with the colonists against the British. The other confederacy nations sided with the British.

The Six Iroquois Nations

After the Tuscarora Indians of present-day North Carolina and South Carolina lost almost all their land to European colonists in the early 1700s, the Oneida and the Cayuga Nations welcomed the Tuscaroras into their villages. They provided land, shelter, and food. In 1715, Tuscarora became the sixth nation in the Iroquois Confederacy.

In this woodcut by a European-American artist, British General Burgoyne is shown talking to Native Americans from different tribes, trying to convince them to fight on the side of the British.

Polly Cooper

During one brutally cold winter of the American Revolution, General George Washington's soldiers at Valley Forge, Pennsylvania, nearly starved. Oneida Chief Skenandoah and Oneida villagers traveled many miles to take the men bags of corn. One Oneida, Polly Cooper, taught them how to prepare the corn. General George Washington (who later became the first president of the United States) tried to pay her for her help, but she refused. To thank and honor her, General Washington's wife, Martha, bought Polly a shawl and bonnet, which the Oneida people still have.

Many Oneidas fought bravely during the Revolutionary War. During the August 6, 1777, Battle of Oriskany in present-day Oneida County, New York, an Oneida named Honyere Tehawenkarogwen continued firing his gun at the British, even after sustaining an injury. While he and nearly five hundred other Oneidas and colonists died in the bloody battle, they were able to stop two British forces from meeting up with each other. This victory helped prevent the British from winning the war.

Oneidas Lose Nearly All Their Land

Following the Revolutionary War, the former colonies grew fast, and settlers were eager to grab the Oneidas' land. The newly formed U.S. government signed the 1794 **Treaty** of Canandaigua with the Oneidas, assuring them they could keep control of their 6 million acres (2.5 million ha) of land in New York.

Despite the federal treaty, New York State made more than thirty fake land treaties with the Oneidas that took their land away. The largest loss took place in 1788 when the Oneida Nation signed the Treaty of Fort Schuyler, believing they were **leasing** 5 million acres (2 million ha) of land to New York State. Instead, they were selling it. In less than sixty years, from the late 1700s to the mid-1800s, the Oneidas' land base shrank to a mere 32 acres (13 ha).

Leaving New York

Between 1821 and 1822, some of the Oneidas paid the Menominee and Winnebago Indians for joint use of 5 million acres (2 million ha) of land along both sides of the Fox River in what is now Wisconsin. In the 1830s, about 650 Oneidas left their homeland for Wisconsin. In 1840, a small group of Oneidas moved to the banks of the Thames River in Ontario, Canada, while another group of about 430 Oneidas moved to Brantford, Ontario, where they bought 5,000 acres (2,000 ha) of land.

Chief Bread, shown here with his wife, led a group of Oneidas from present-day New York to what is now Wisconsin in the early 1800s.

Mary Cornelius Winder

Even though their New York homeland had shrunk to only 32 acres (13 ha) by the early 1800s, a number of Oneidas refused to move to Wisconsin or Canada. One of their **descendants**, Mary Cornelius Winder, spent much of her life fighting for a return of the Oneida's New York lands. A mother of eleven children, storekeeper, and artisan, she wrote letter after letter to the federal government from the 1920s through the early 1950s, asking it to honor its treaties with the Oneida Nation.

Loss of Land for the Wisconsin Oneidas

In 1827, shortly after the Oneida group had moved to Wisconsin, the Menominees and Winnebagos agreed to a treaty with the federal government that reduced the 5 million acres of land that the Oneidas had paid to live on with them. By 1838, the Oneidas' new lands had shrunk to only 65,000 acres (26,300 ha).

Even that land, however, did not remain within the Wisconsin Oneidas' control for long. The General Allotment Act of 1887 transferred Oneida **reservation** lands held by the whole tribe into the hands of individuals. By dividing the **communal** land, the U.S. government had hoped to end what remained of Native American tradition, **culture**, and government. When the government taxed these new individual owners, few understood how and when they should pay their taxes. Many Wisconsin Oneidas missed deadlines and were forced to sell their land to

Meeting in Ontario, Canada, in 1871, the Iroquois Confederacy Council made decisions that benefited all people within the confederacy's six nations. Iroquois leaders are still supposed to base each decision on its effect on peace, the natural world, and the children of the future.

MT. PLEASANT INDIAN SCHOOL
GRADUATING. CLASS. 1911 *

Graduating from high school was a huge accomplishment for many teens in the early 1900s. In 1911, however, it also meant these Oneida and other Indian students were forced to give up their traditional culture, clothing, and language.

settle their debts. By 1924, the 65,000-acre Wisconsin Oneida Reservation had shrunk to a few hundred acres.

Recovering Land and Strength

Further land loss for the Wisconsin Oneidas was halted when Congress passed the Indian Reorganization Act of 1934. This law helped the Wisconsin Oneidas draft a **constitution** and establish a government that was able to buy 1,270 acres (515 ha) of land in 1937 for the Wisconsin Oneidas.

Farming this land, however, did not produce much profit, and the **Great Depression** of the late 1920s and early 1930s put many Wisconsin Oneidas out of the few nonfarming jobs they held. Most people had little money and lived in poor housing. Many suffered from ill health. Despite these problems, the Wisconsin Oneidas slowly regained strength. By the 1970s, the Wisconsin Oneida government had won federal grants that they used to build schools, health clinics, and a youth center.

Traditional Way of Life

A Hearty Mealtime

A traditional Oneida meal must have satisfied the hungriest of appetites. As described by a Dutch trader who visited the Oneidas in 1634, a typical meal included corn-based dishes such as cornbread with chestnuts and cornmeal mush, baked and boiled pumpkins, meats, fish, and beans, as well as dried strawberries and blueberries.

Baked cornbread is one of many healthful dishes the Oneidas made from corn.

A Land of Plenty

The Oneida homeland produced plenty of food for its people. Men hunted the many deer, wild turkeys, rabbits, and other small game that roamed the fields and forests, while women and children planted and harvested gardens that yielded three main crops — corn, beans, and squash. Because the Oneidas considered the environment a part of their family, they called these crops the three sisters. Women and children also gathered berries, nuts, and greens to round out their diet.

The Oneidas practiced slash-and-burn farming; they cleared and burned off an area and then planted. When the soil became less fertile, or able to support crops, they simply moved, leaving one village and starting another.

The streams and rivers emptying into Lake Ontario and the St. Lawrence River held lots of

Oneida longhouses showed that the people valued harmony and balance. The graceful arc of bent, young trees form an oval roof, while straight trees provide a contrast.

salmon and other fish that the men killed with spears. The men also fished in Oneida Lake as well as the Mohawk, Oswego, and Oneida Rivers.

A Home for All

Along streams or lakes where they found fertile land, the Oneidas built their villages of longhouses from elm trees. First, they stripped and dried the bark. Then they drove long, thick branches upright into the ground. These branches formed the sides of the house. The Oneidas bent other branches over the side branches to frame the roof. After tying both sets of branches together with young, flexible trees, they covered the house with the dried bark. Most longhouses stood about 18 feet (5.5 meters) high but could vary in length from 40 to 300 feet (12 to 91 m), depending on the number of families housed within. Doors were placed at both ends of the longhouses.

Each family had its own 20-foot (6-m) section along one side of the longhouse with sleeping bunks and shelves that held clothes, baskets, and household items. Cooking fires lined the center aisle of the longhouses every 20 feet (6 m). Families living across the aisle from each other shared a fire. Roof holes above the fire pits let the smoke escape.

Clan Connections

All members of the village belonged to one of three clans — Wolf, Bear, or Turtle. Clan membership depended on the mother. All children born of a Wolf Clan mother belonged to the Wolf Clan. When the Wolf Clan girls grew up, they married someone from outside their clan. Their children, however, remained Wolf clan members. When boys grew up and married, they, too, had to marry someone outside their clan. The children of these marriages belonged to the mother's clan.

The three eldest women of each of the three clans served as clan leaders. They watched over all the clan's families, helping to settle family disputes and choose marriage partners for young women and men. They also chose the male chiefs, or sachems, who represented their clan in village councils and in

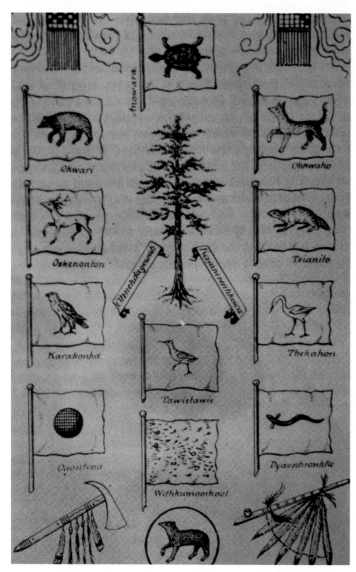

Named after water, land, and sky animals that give special help to people, clans are made up of family groups sharing the same female ancestors. Oneidas belonged to one of three clans — the Bear, the Wolf, and the Turtle — shown on this Iroquois clan chart.

Women, such as Mary Ann Bread shown here, play an important role in Oneida tribal life and are considered equal to men. Bread, daughter of Chief Daniel Bread, earned a degree in nursing and was a member of the Oneida Women's Guild.

the Iroquois Confederacy. If the clan mothers decided that the chiefs were not fulfilling their responsibilities, they could replace the chiefs with new chiefs.

The Iroquois Confederacy

Respected women leaders from each of the three Oneida clans chose the nine Oneida chiefs who represented the Oneidas in the Iroquois Confederacy. A peacekeeping group, the Confederacy's council was made up fifty sachems — nine Mohawk, nine Oneida, fourteen Onondaga, ten Cayuga, and eight Seneca chiefs. Complex voting and decision-making procedures prevented one nation from dominating another.

The Rhythm of Life

Iroquois Indians made useful and decorative baskets from a variety of grasses and cornhusks. Some versions of the Iroquois creation story say that Sky Woman grabbed a strawberry plant as she fell toward the earth. Perhaps this is why the basket maker wove a strawberry design into her basket.

Villagers devoted much of their time to the important tasks upon which life depended — hunting, gathering, growing, harvesting, and fixing food. Making shelters and clothing took time as well. Until the Oneida people traded fur for European cloth in the 1600s, Oneida women made clothing from deerskins; it took seventeen skins to make enough clothing for a family of five. Both men and women wove corn husks, grasses, and bark into beautiful and useful storage baskets.

Time remained, however, for fun and games. Long before the Europeans arrived in North America, the Oneidas played *ga lahs*, a game now known as lacrosse. Hundreds of players would race across mile-long fields, using hickory-wood sticks with rawhide pockets to toss and catch wooden balls.

When the elder men and women told stories, all family members, including the children, listened. Stories kept history alive and made people feel connected.

Oneida Beliefs

The Oneidas believed that a generous Creator had blessed them with many gifts, including Mother Earth and all that she provided. Each and every child was considered a gift from the

~~~ And the Moral of the Story Is . . . ~~~

Some stories, such as one about the fox and the mice, taught lessons. Two mice kept fighting about how to divide a piece of cheese. Each mouse wanted an equal share. When a fox divided it for them, the mice said the pieces were not the same. As the fox kept eating bites from each piece, trying to make them equal, the mice insisted they were not. Finally, the cheese was gone. The fox had eaten it all. The lesson? People who don't learn to share can end up with nothing!

Creator. The Oneidas never spanked or used physical force to punish their children. With gentle guidance, children learned to respect their elders and to voice their own opinions. The Oneidas believed that the Creator gave every child a special gift. Parents were told to watch for and nurture these gifts. If a girl showed a love for music, for example, her parents encouraged her to make instruments or sing and dance.

To express their thanks for the Creator's gifts, the Oneidas held ceremonies throughout the year. Many ceremonies were connected with the change of seasons. After Mother Earth had

Oneida ceremonies honor the land's bounty, both in their traditional lands and in their new home in Wisconsin. In fall, the colorful trees around the Fox River in Wisconsin resemble those of their New York homelands.

During their traditional ceremonies, Iroquois dancers shake colorful rattles made of shells and feathers. Songs and dances celebrate the gifts of life and an ancient heritage.

The Seven Dancers

According to a traditional tale told by the Oneidas, after seven Iroquois children formed a secret group, their parents used violence to try to break it up. The children sang a sacred and powerful song that lifted them from the earth to the stars. The lonely parents promised the children that if they returned, they would never hit them again. One child tried to return, but he fell and became a shooting star. The other children remained in the heavens, forming a **constellation**. These stars remind Oneida parents to treat their children gently, as the Creator had intended.

taken a long winter nap, the Oneida people thanked her for awakening with the Midwinter Ceremony, which lasted up to eight days. When the sugar maple sap began to flow in early spring, the Maple Ceremony allowed people to again give thanks — to the blood of the tree for giving nourishment to the people. Oneida women made syrup from the sap. During the early spring Seed or Planting Ceremony, the Oneidas expressed their thanks to the Creator for the seeds from which a bounty of crops would grow.

Ceremonies began with prayers of thanks, followed by traditional songs and dances. Rattles, made from turtle shells and gourds, helped the dancers and singers keep tempo. Each man, woman, and child who attended these ceremonies played an equal and valued role, lending voice to a communal chorus of thanks and celebration.

An Equal Role for All

Women and men were considered equal partners. As the givers of life, women exercised responsibility for all things that grew. The men cleared the fields, but the women decided when to plant the seeds and cared for and harvested the crops. Women also tended the young children. Men provided comfort and security by building longhouses, making fires, fighting enemies, and hunting for food.

Both women and men taught children the skills they needed for adulthood. While mothers busied themselves with young children, older aunts and grandmothers often taught the older girls how to sew and cook. While young fathers went hunting, older uncles or grandfathers would teach the boys how to detect upcoming weather changes or how to fashion bows and spears from wood — skills needed for hunting and tracking.

Just as they used natural materials to build their homes, the Oneidas used such materials to make toys for the children. This doll is made from deer-skin. It shows how traditional Oneidas separated animal fur from skin so both parts could be used.

Today

The Oneidas have three nations throughout North America: Oneida of Wisconsin, Oneida of the Thames, and Oneida of New York. While many Oneidas live on national reserves, including the Six Nations Reserve for members of the Iroquois Confederacy, others live throughout the United States and Canada.

The Strong Grow Stronger

After years of economic hard times, many residents of Oneida County and the Mohawk Valley of central New York State are prospering. Their good fortune is due, in large part, to efforts of the Oneida Nation. The Oneida-owned Turning Stone **Casino** Resort in Verona, New York, as well as fifteen other Oneida-owned businesses employ nearly four thousand people, some of whom are Native Americans. Profits from these businesses fund more than sixty programs, including housing and health services that support members of the Oneida Nation. A lacrosse and softball field as well as a children and elders center — where elders teach the children Oneida traditions, language, and history — help the Oneidas stay united as a people and keep traditions alive.

Wisconsin Oneidas: A Healthy Community

Hoping to use its profits to help its people, the Wisconsin Oneida entered the gambling industry in 1976. Profits from bingo games run by a few volunteers paid for a new community recreation center. After the Indian Gaming Regulatory Act of 1988 recognized the right of tribal governments to run and keep the profits from gambling casinos, the Wisconsin Oneidas expanded

The Oneida Nation of Wisconsin's main Oneida Bingo and Casino facility stays open twenty-four hours a day, seven days a week. In 1976, the first Wisconsin Oneida bingo game made $85 in profits. Today, the enterprise earns millions of dollars in profits that help pay for the nation's health, educational, and cultural programs.

their efforts into a multimillion dollar enterprise. Gaming profits fund **social services** and schools, create businesses, and allow the nation to buy back Wisconsin Oneida land.

In 2004, the Oneida Tribe of Wisconsin employed more people than any other business in northeastern Wisconsin. About three thousand people worked for the nation; nearly half of them are Oneidas. The tribe has repurchased more than 25 percent of their original 65,000 acres (26,300 ha); as of 2004, reservation land totaled nearly 17,000 acres (6,900 ha).

To help its long-range goal of educating future leaders, the Oneida Tribe of Wisconsin opened a tribal school in 1979. The students learn about their Oneida heritage and culture as well as reading, mathematics, science, and social studies. Five of the twenty remaining **fluent** Wisconsin Oneida elders teach the Oneida language to schoolchildren. The tribe provides a number of **scholarships** that help families cover expenses for education beyond high school. Summer job-training programs for teenagers teach job-finding and other useful employment skills.

The Oneida Tribe of Wisconsin also offers extensive health and social services for people who suffer from ill health, drug and alcohol abuse, and other problems. A system of assisted living centers and nursing homes helps take care of Oneida elders.

Some of the Wisconsin Oneidas' thriving businesses include the Oneida Radisson Hotel in Green Bay, Wisconsin, which houses a gift shop, and conference center. In 2003, the Oneidas formed a business partnership called the Four Fires. The Oneidas' partners include the Forest County Potawatomi Community of Wisconsin and two tribes from southern California — the San Manuel Band of Mission Indians and the Viejas Band of Kamewayy Indians. Their first business venture is the construction of a Marriott Residence Inn in Washington, D.C.

To keep the Oneida language alive, Oneida Nations run language classes. The Wisconsin Oneida Nation recognizes Oneida-speaking elders as national treasures. A training program for teachers will ensure that youth understand and speak the language.

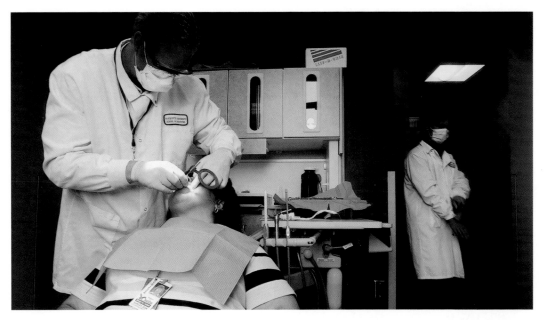

The Wisconsin Oneida Nation has turned casino profits into badly needed health facilities and services for its people. In this reservation-based, modern facility built in 2003, a dentist works on a member's teeth.

Traditions Still Honored

With help from the Oneida Tribe's Arts Program, the Wisconsin Oneida still keep the old traditions young. Art program funds allowed Wisconsin Oneida muralist Sharon Sarnowski to paint a

～～～ Indian Community School ～～～

A private, intertribal school, the Indian Community School in Milwaukee, Wisconsin, enrolls about 360 children. Ninety of the children are Oneida. In addition to learning traditional subjects such as math and science, students learn core Native American values of bravery, love, truth, wisdom, humility, loyalty, and respect. Their education also focuses on Indian spirituality, language, and ceremonies. Teachers believe that they are counselors of their children for all time.

Dancers from a Wisconsin Oneida Nation troupe perform at school and civic events throughout northeastern Wisconsin.

20-foot (96-m), turtle-shaped lunar calendar in the Norbert Hill Center in Oneida, Wisconsin. Throughout the year, the arts program brings American Indian musicians and writers who perform to enthusiastic audiences in the community. The arts group also sponsors writing workshops as well as fry bread contests and dances, where young and old Oneidas perform Native jigging to the sounds of old-time fiddles.

Handcrafted from white pine logs, the Oneida Nation's Shako:wi Cultural Center near Syracuse, New York, displays many traditional items such as baskets and rattles. It also serves as a gathering place for Oneidas who wish to learn and practice traditional arts.

Showcasing Talents

To increase the presence of Indians on American television screens, Native American actor and producer Sonny Skyhawk started the Oneida Nation's Four Directions talent search. Open to American Indian and First Nation (Canadian Indian) people interested in showcasing their acting, comedy, and writing talents, the search ended in 2003. Bruce King of Santa Fe, New Mexico, and a member of the Oneida Tribe of Wisconsin won for his screenplays "The Woods Will Harbor" and "Evening at the Warbonnet."

Students at the University of Wisconsin, Madison, can take a class with poet and scholar Roberta Hill, Ph.D., a member of the Oneida Nation of Wisconsin. Hill teaches writing and American Indian Studies classes. She is also writing a biography of her grandmother, R. L. Rosa Minoka-Hill, who became a doctor on the Wisconsin Oneida Reservation in the early 1900s.

A Sturdy Culture

After withstanding tremendous losses over thousands of years, the Oneida people remain proud of their history, traditions, and ability to thrive. Many Oneidas continue to participate in ceremonies that uphold ancient traditions honoring Mother Earth and all her gifts. By treating the earth and all that springs from her with respect, the Oneidas uphold their responsibility for ensuring the well-being of the next seven generations.

When Oneida elders tell the creation story, Oneida children learn that although the world contains both dark and good forces, the good forces **prevail** — just as the Oneida people have prevailed.

The Oneida Nation treasures its children. The nation's vision for the future includes respect for cultural traditions such as ceremony and dance.

Graham Greene, an Oneida Screen and Television Star

Actor Graham Greene, an Oneida born on the Six Nations Reserve in Ontario, Canada, won fame portraying Kicking Bird, friend to actor Kevin Costner in the 1990 movie *Dances with Wolves.* He has also appeared on many television shows, including *Murder, She Wrote* and *The Red Green Show.*

Well-known film and TV actor Graham Greene reads from the Declaration of Independence during a July 4 celebration.

Time Line

1142	The Oneida, Mohawk, Onondaga, Cayuga, and Seneca Nations form the Iroquois League or Confederacy to put an end to war.
1400s	Oneida villages spread through 6 million acres (2.5 million hectares) of central New York.
late 1500s–1700s	The Oneidas trade furs and hides for metal pots, metal tools, cloth, and beads brought to North America by the Europeans.
1634	Measles and smallpox epidemics kill thousands of Oneidas and their Iroquois neighbors.
1715	After losing their land to colonists, the Tuscarora Indians from present-day North Carolina and South Carolina move to Oneida country and become the sixth nation in the Iroquois Confederacy.
1766	Missionary Samuel Kirkland urges Oneidas to give up their native customs and replace them with white people's customs.
1775–83	Revolutionary War; many Oneida warriors fight against the British.
1788	By signing the Treaty of Fort Schuyler, the Oneidas give up nearly all their land to New York State.
1822–23	Many Oneidas move to the Green Bay, Wisconsin, area.
1887	General Allotment Act transfers Wisconsin Oneida-held lands into hands of individuals.
1934	Indian Reorganization Act helps Wisconsin Oneidas draft a constitution and establish a government.
1970s	The Wisconsin Oneidas win federal monies that help them build schools and health clinics.
1988	Wisconsin Oneidas start expanding their gambling industry into a multimillion-dollar enterprise.
1993	Oneida Nation of New York opens Turning Stone Casino.
2004	Oneida Nation of Wisconsin employs more people than any other business in northeastern Wisconsin. The Oneida Nation of New York employs nearly four thousand people, restoring economic health to reservation lands.

Glossary

ancestors: people from whom an individual or group is descended

casino: a building that has slot machines and other gambling games.

clan: a group of related families.

communal: owned by a group of people rather than by individuals.

confederacy: a group of people, countries, or states united for a common purpose.

constellation: a group of stars that look like they form an image.

constitution: the basic laws and principles of a nation that outline the powers of the government and the rights of the people.

culture: the arts, beliefs, and customs that form a people's way of life.

descendants: all of the children and children's children of an individual or group; those who come after.

enrolled: registered with a tribe, school, or other organization.

fluent: able to easily speak a specific language.

Great Depression: the period from 1929 to 1939, when people lost their jobs, homes, farms, and businesses.

immunity: protection from a disease.

leasing: renting land or rights to someone; the owner keeps ownership of the land but allows someone to use it in exchange for money.

nation: people who have their own customs, laws, and land separate from other nations or peoples.

neutral: not taking sides in an argument.

prevail: to triumph or win; to be effective.

reservation/reserve: land set aside by the U.S. or Canadian government for specific Indian tribes to live on.

sacred: set apart for religious purposes.

scholarships: money for students to attend a school or college.

social services: services provided by the government or other organizations to help the poor, needy, or sick.

treaty: an agreement among two or more nations.

More Resources

Web Sites:

http://www.carnegiemuseums.org/cmnh/exhibits/north-south-east-west/iroquois Describes the Oneidas' and other Iroquois nations' traditional relationship with animals as well as their ability to survive after the fur trade ended.

http://www.oneida-nation.net New York Oneida Nation news and events as well as cultural and historical information make this an informative site. Take an online tour of the Shako:wi Cultural Center to see beaded handbags, corn-husk dolls, wampum belts, and wood-splint baskets.

http://www.oneida-nation.net/irolegends.html Read the story that tells why corn-husk dolls have no face and other traditional tales.

http://www.oneidanation.org Read the history of the wolf, bear, and turtle clans as well as of the homelands on the Wisconsin Oneida Nation's web site.

Books:

Houghton, Gillian. *The Oneida of Wisconsin.* Powerkids Press, 2003.

Hoyt-Goldsmith, Diane. *Lacrosse: The National Game of the Iroquois.* Holiday House, 1998.

Press, Petra. *The Iroquois.* Compass Point Books, 2001.

Trottier, Maxine. *By the Standing Stone.* Fitzhenry & Whiteside, 2001.

Underwood, Paula. *Franklin Listens When I Speak: Tellings of the Friendship between Benjamin Franklin and Skenandoah, an Oneida Chief.* Tribe of Two Presses, The LearningWay Company, 1997.

Things to Think About and Do

Defend Land Claims

Pretend you are a lawyer. Write two reasons to give a judge explaining why New York State should return Oneida land to the Oneidas.

Prepare a Traditional Dish

Visit the Wisconsin Oneida Nation's web site to find a recipe for succotash, a traditional Oneida dish. With adult help, fix the succotash and tell your family why Oneida called corn, beans, and squash the three sisters.

Draw a Picture

Think about how the Oneidas made their longhouses and write down the steps. Then draw a picture of the outside of a longhouse.

Writing for the Sports Pages

Pretend that you are a sportswriter, and write a short article telling how today's game of lacrosse resembles the game played by traditional Oneidas.

Imagine

An Oneida musical group called the Little Big Band blends Native American, country, and rock music. Their songs express good feelings about being a Native American. Think of three feelings an Oneida might have about his or her identity and discuss them in a group.

Index